Oh the wonders of music

Oh, how the wonders of music
transport me to an indescribable dimension
with feelings difficult to define
and places I fail to mention

Oh, how the wonders of music
trap me in a world of my own
yet a world that cannot be made
without the ones that I know

Oh, how the wonders of music
speak my failed words
we realise it's an intimate relation
as the power of words cannot be mistaken

Oh, how the wonders of music
take me to these worlds
to give a sincere understanding
of what surrounds oneself

Oh, how the wonders of music
provide an infinite serenity to the soul
and warmth to the heart
I think music
is my favourite kind of art

My Painting and Yours

by

Tess Lina Aiteouakrim

Conscious Dreams
PUBLISHING

My Painting and Yours

Copyright © 2023 Tess Lina Aiteouakrim

First Printed in United Kingdom 2023

Published by Conscious Dreams Publishing
www.consciousdreamspublishing.com

Photo Illustration by Sean Murphy

Book Interior and E-book Design by Amit Dey

ISBN: 978-1-915522-53-5

To everyone who has *been*
and *are* a part of my life

Life is a painting.
You are the paint and brush.
Adding unconscious marks at every moment,
brushing the colours with your passions,
sketching the emotions, to only realise
their permanence after all.
Letting moments of light shine through,
fading the feelings and smudging those scenes.
As you let life's logic lead you into the unknown,
you're creating a glorious canvas of everything
there is to know.

Contents

How fortuitous it is
that life has chosen us
how great it is
to be alive
but how spectacular it is
to be living

CREATIVE COLOURS

The safety net

Her rays are the mesh
intersected through the windows
of my soul
lighting my inner dull
triggering the bloom
of the hopeless love
I have for you
but who am I referring to?
her warmth makes me giddy
her warmth sets my mind free
contenting me
making me believe
that I can achieve
and makes me relieve
that she's still there
when it's clouding
foggy or misty
like my mind is sometimes
but still melts my thoughts
the ones that shouldn't pass by

Distance is never an issue
93 million miles
and she still smiles
when she radiates me
triggering home
within my lone
she glistens
as she kisses
every part of me that I cannot see
reminding that beauty is natural
she shouts
'I am powerful
and so are thee'
as she dries the tears
running down my face
whilst she sets
I reminisce of you
before I fall
into the pool
of dusk

Piano parachute

They ask "what's a piano parachute?"
I say "to slow the descent, so I can
see through the fall"
they ask "why do you want to see yourself falling?"
I say "the sites are simply enthralling,
how could you miss this unique view,
it's certainly one that your shoes cannot walk you through"

They ask "why do you wear it when you're not even
descending?"
I say "if we are not falling, we are floating
if we are not floating, we are sinking
if we are not sinking, we are swinging
back and forth, up and down
you deserve to feel
even at places you cannot be found"

They say "it doesn't make sense"
I say "it does;
your heart doesn't stop beating
your mind doesn't stop thinking

your lungs don't stop inhaling the air
as you fly through the highs and lows
how the piano can articulate
the depths of your descent
and indeed heighten the heights
the keys are the streets to the soul
the melodies are the paths to the heart"

They say "don't be so daft"
I say "how mad I ever could be
to finally understand
the passions I couldn't fathom
to realise the truths behind all these atoms
the piano guided me to a beauty
few there must have been
so how can I ever miss a rare view
that was meant to be seen"

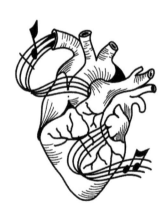

Jeff Buckley

His voice stabs me in the heart
with a knife made of flowers
how the petals wrap me in parts
the roots pull me with powers
deepening my love for the arts
dragging me to a depth for hours
how passion can tear you apart
and a beauty not yours, or mine, but ours.

Contentment within the chaos
a noun but first a verb
a non-existent definition
an essence that cannot effuse
the intertwining of complex themes
the thing we are all trying to seek
because even a touch to the heart
will make you wonder for this art
the souls sparkle to safety
and the mind marvels achingly
the force that fights you to stay
the energy propelling your day
a life without it, is a life not lived
yet it creeps in soundly
as your heart beats profoundly
because there are no boundaries
letting the adventure begin...

—love

The Rose

May this be the first poem
for many to come
since there aren't enough words in the dictionary
to describe how thankful I am
to call you my mum

Grounded, powerful
and certainly strong willed
whatever you put your mind to
you'll undoubtedly fulfil
something intrinsic, built within
with roots deep but never so thin
yet so fragile and beautiful
and you never fail to show
through the wise words
you give your children
that people too must rise and fall
in order to grow

You are a rose, singular and gleam
a sturdy stem, thorns by your side
made from the pain and experiences
you had to hide behind your eyes

Your petals pierced with colour
rich and profound
like the shell to your heart
but with a touch so gentle, soft and kind
is the true reflection of what hides inside

Your essence effuses love and care
no wonder everyone craves
to be in the same air
but even those who try to pick your petals
have eventually realised
that your scent never settles

How the Rose can be one of a kind
surfing the rain
and embracing all the sunshine
how the Rose can be tough and tender
surviving the storms
and any harsher weather

Grateful, proud and luckiest I can be
since the Rose isn't one
that just grows on trees
but one that will forever be close to my heart
because the Rose isn't just anyone
but my one, and only mum

(Sound) Waves

Sensing
the sensitivity
as the splashes
swash the soul

Ocean motion
the governor
of emotions
but it's the scream
of the wind
causing the crashes
within

Taken through the currents
gulped by the gulf stream
a storm may follow
but we swim its seams

Melancholic microplastics
scratch the vinyl

like a common friend
reminding us
of the sounds of them

Smiling through the drown
surfing the musical sounds
it's art that keeps us going
it's the force that keeps us flowing
and we don't need anything else
because art comes free
and too is the strength
which sets us free

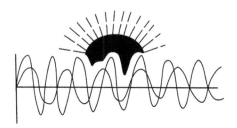

Only the sun

The sparkle
from my eye
is activated
by your radiation
how I glimmer
with no hesitations
hope harnesses me
as my mind runs free

How this is only
the sun
and not a soul
I think the sun
will melt me
when I finally
meet a soul

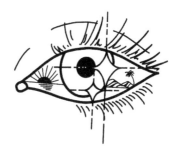

Creative corner

Veins bleed melancholia
a heart hefty with passion
my corner of creativity
cradled by black and white keys
and with substantive strings
taken overseas
carried with infinite reasons
to be beside me

My corner of creation
the safest vertex there can be
captures all the tears
stops me drowning
from my heart
which soundly
and softly
beats melancholy

Immersed

You are the single leaf
through the gust of wind
living an ageless life
with each breath you take
drowning in the depths of your mistakes
guided by the stars without hesitation
their light slices through your veins
as they battle with the sun's rays
but you cannot feel, you cannot see
how your blood rushes
like the sea of a tsunami
drenching you in intimacy
creating your symphony
of wonder and mystery

Your heart is racing
from the shadows you've created
their darkness pulls far from beneath
trapping you as you fall to your feet
suffocating, welling, exhilarating it may be

and these feelings are making you rather thirsty
but as you quench your thirst with a glassful of tears
the shadows vanish
erasing any of those fears

Your body flowing, heart tumbling
your body rolling, heart flying
your body numb, heart shattered
your body free, heart scattered
cursive outlines, paths undesigned
always leading to those feelings
which cannot be defined

HEAVY
STROKES

She was lost
I was searching
but she did not want
to be found.

The deep ocean

They say the ocean
is the deeper than the highest mountain
and you said we can climb up it together
but you always knew I was a swimmer

I was swimming to a depth you couldn't reach
because I surpassed that mountain far from beneath
as I looked up and down, back and around
I couldn't see you
not even a glimpse
it seemed you lived in the shallows

I stopped, I waited
but I couldn't tread for so long
because the waves grew too strong
so I had to keep going
and let my tears clear the salt from my eyes
because they were stinging deep inside

My heart sunk, but I had to stay afloat
to swim from the current
that was coming to me so close
the cold sliced though
and the oceans grew deeper
and it shouldn't have gotten any easier
but I grew stronger
than ever before
despite feeling
so, so sore

Throughout your life things change.

Remember, these 'things'
can mean people too.

Dull thoughts
ears blind
a fuelless fire
is still a struggle to find

Trails are an empty house
dead ends are home
a crossroad is my only friend
handing an illegible map to follow

A warm hug
from the gloomy clouds above
that was a false encounter
since the cold is stabbing my heart

Intoxicated tear ducts
it stings to cry
grey is my favourite colour
it's all I can see

Although, it's rather tempting
to find the blue
and ask
who are you? where are you?

—You are lost

Looking back

Indeed, you made my heart throb
with joy, care and love
how we embraced each other over the years
with all the experiences we shared

Walking through our paths
with a hand to hold along the way
appreciating our differences
not just in our appearances
having a balance that worked out
I was there for you
you were there for me
no matter what the circumstances would've been
but through the high and lows
from parties to the school trips
watching the sunsets before they dipped
catching the tears as they started falling
coffee dates and advice calling
late night walks
and those deep talks

Indeed, you made my heart throb
with affection, solicitude and mystification
I embraced you over the years
as we confided to our fears

From the rare spontaneous trips
holding onto those nights before they slipped
cherishing the moments when trees waved hello
as we sat on those benches
we were on the same page
at least I thought that,
change is inevitable though
and you proved that

Indeed, you made my heart throb
with distress, anguish and strain
certainly my heart had bled
with a cut, stab or jab
a scar was made
from the dent you engraved
I would never have thought that
you'll just leave
like nothing ever happened

—Look back; read it backwards

If it still hurts
that's okay.

Because
it truly meant something

at least to you.

Vacant call

I had a friend
15 years to end
a dimension
to connect
like a wire attached
to our hearts
ready to call
at any time
to talk at any depth
despair or lightness
to chest tightness
a phone call away
ready to take
whatever was to come
someone to talk to
is now hollow
void
is where
my phone rings
empty

the air is
I breathe
as I talk
to myself
since
'I'
is all I got
it seems
that my depths
have dragged me
to places
people cannot reach
but I know
there are few
out there
I just don't know
where

I'm on the verge
of tears
I'm going to take
a shower

— *A quick decision*

Out of touch

A head too heavy
to carry
a thought a kilogram
a wonder a tonne
a murmur of lost
an inhale of fuzz
from a gush of wind
of your tornado above

Eyes touching the streets
sights of your feet
rock bottom
is where your heart beats

Shoulders are home
for the family of weight
but it's rather audacious
how they slump
leaving no rooms capacious

Weight has left
but burdens are birthed
into the sinking home
you heave afloat

A blink
is insufficient
to clear your vision
blur is now abode
to mind and body alone

But mind is lost
and body has strayed
it seems that
they have parted ways

Sometimes
you got to listen to your body
and walk away
you deserve to save your heart
not let it decay

INDIRECT
LIGHT

Butterfly cage

I have a little cage inside of me
full of butterflies
which are made of love and care
each day another butterfly enters the cage
but they are waiting to be released
to liberate that immense love and care

But the cage is only so big
and with each day it seems these butterflies
are beginning to suffocate
they have been waiting ever so patiently
yet they have found a way to survive
lucky for them, the air by which they breathe
is not made of oxygen

but is made of hope

I only knew as much of him as he knew me
which was hardly a lot
but was enough
to know that
he was
rare.

Same track, different feet

Same track, different feet
it felt like we were walking a similar road
with a distance that was unknown

We were so different
yet your trail felt so familiar
maybe our paths crossed only once
at a time when my heart was being dented
by a person who I thought was a friend

Same track, different feet
how we get this strange feeling
rarely by the people we meet

How someone can provide comfort
when they don't even know
by the little things, like a helping hand
or explaining that page we don't understand

Developed feelings unconsciously
just from a face of familiarity
but it was a face unknown
because I didn't really know you
in fact, I didn't know you at all

Same track, different feet
it's funny really
because I think we lived
across the same street

But you were ahead
and I was behind
you didn't slow down
and neither did I
you never stopped
and I never sped
it seems our tracks
never
met

It seems like we live

in a little big world

It's going

As I think once again
I realise the thoughts are going
further away, blurred and dismayed
oh how I wish this day finally came
but it's not a day, a week or four
but a matter of time before the thoughts can thaw

Temperatures rise but then they drop
how I imagined my thoughts were going
but
then
they
stopped
frozen and solid the thoughts sat still
the images reminding me what could've been
as I began to think that these were deleted scenes

But it takes time for summer to arrive
the temperatures can rise and the sun shines
I guess now the sun is a reflection of my thoughts

the rays are long but can never be caught
this new distance is one to last
yet still melting the thoughts if they ever pass

As I think once again
the thoughts are nearly gone
a fuzzy image, a haze, maybe a very long gaze
a lost memory, but how can that ever be true
because it seems that my world
never
chose
you

You need to let go

You need to let go
you need to let go
don't fall into shadows of your past
or holding those thoughts if they pass

You need to let go
you need to let go
live in the present, take this gift
stop staying behind to only drown in that mist

You need to let go
you need to let go
of what could've been
this fantasy is frazzling you
and stabbing you falsely

You need to let go
you need to let go
a lost love or a hidden dream
don't be fooled

hope is the only thing
that takes this lead

You need to let go
as your face is about to sadden
you need to let go
because nothing ever happened
you need to let go
of holding onto this phantom
that's acting as a remote distraction
reminiscing the past interactions
of that one-sided attraction

You need to let go
nothing will happen
you are here
and they'll never be near
for you to hear

nothing

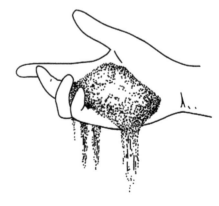

You can tell the difference
when the sparkle of a gem
is amongst the dull of rocks
little did you expect to find one
when you were never searching

You grab the gem
but with hands of butter

I guess what matters
is what remains
even if it's just
the glister from your eyes
that stays
forever

One day you'll look
back and laugh

That thought flared
but I smiled
extinguishing
whatever that was there

Silly is now sane
but sane was never silly
because feelings were felt
and wonders were never dealt

An evanescent rarity
is what you were
like a diamond
held in a hand of grease

I was prescribed with laughter
it's the best medicine they say
even if it was a placebo
I'm fully dosed everyday

I know a part of my heart
will forever be waiting in your silence
but laughter patched that part
and muted the scream of 'what if'

Yesterday or one day
somewhere or here
you'll look back and laugh
with the flutter in your heart
which smiles too
and reminds you
that you are free

Hug me

Distance was always an issue for me
scenes were only birthed from the mind
created by my pathetic curiosity inside
I hugged you
as I wrapped a single arm around you
you gripped me with both
I knew it was a dream
and you didn't
I wanted to scream
because we never touched
a hug so hollow
is worse than no hug at all
because I knew I'll fall
into your shadows
for how dreams are evil
for a brief escape
knowing they are f*cking fake
but as I wake
I know I'll break
for how there is empty air

beside me
as you never will ever
hug me

The imaginary one

Straggling screams
from my heart
waver away
like a flame
before it goes astray

My soul sings
for another
like birds on a tree
but now it dangles
and has cuts
through its seams
from the cry
of my heart
as hopeless love
bursts my veins

But my eyes still gleam
when I feel
the breeze
from the imaginary one

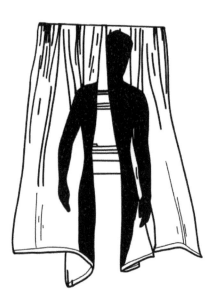

Fantasies
are not like dreams
they don't come true

      They don't come true.

A lost love

An empty touch
a false hope
a hidden kiss
and nowhere to go

A lost love
or a lonely heart
capturing our thoughts
turning them into art

Wishes and wonders
fantasies and dreams
it seems that love
is the thing
we are all trying to seek

Don't think too hard
don't speak too soon
you'll feel it in your heart
that truths are hidden in art

An empty touch
a false hope
a hidden kiss
and one day
you'll find where to go

PERMANENT SKETCHES

Why do I feel everything so deeply
but it's okay
because I can swim the depths
in the pool of my tears

I had to learn
I had no choice.

Wrong generation

I think I was born in the wrong generation
and we may be on the same page
because we appreciate that ink on the paper
far more than the light from our screens
pulling us in to see these zany teens

I think I was born in the wrong generation
because people took me by surprise
when I said I didn't have that social media app
that nearly everyone uses as a disguise
or dismissing the offer of a vape
as I don't feel like putting my lungs at stake

I think I was born in the wrong generation
because I much rather write love letters to a lover
the fonts created and the words read
give you a serenity to the heart instead
of looking on the screen
where you cannot read the lines in-between

I think I was born in the wrong generation
because I would rather drown
in the depths of my despair
than use a device
to distract and falsely guide me to repair

I think I was born in the wrong generation
because I have an 'old soul', so they say
living in the depths of the oceans
viewing the storms raging free
but it's a tragedy really, since I can understand you
but you cannot understand me

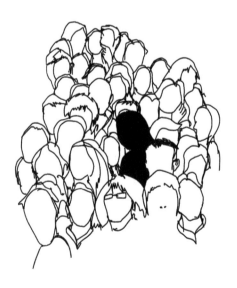

It's a weird thing really
we cannot move it
we cannot hold it
but we can control how we use it
because I guess it's the only thing
which we truly have
until
we
don't

—Time

The window

A portal of escapism for the eyes
despite feeling trapped inside
the colours of the sunset filled my heart
with a sense of wonder for the arts
the blue skies filling me with hope
reminding me that I can actually cope
sometimes the rain poured
but I too felt somewhat restored
behind the grey clouds the sun still shines
and by 8pm the sun will pull my eyes

The sun can shape clouds, change skies
dry the tears from people's eyes
how the reds, oranges, yellows and pinks
made me gaze in awe and simply think
that life too brings us these rich colours
sometimes we may feel we suffer
other times we may feel tougher

we may be filled with love and tender
and how we embraced the splendour
but as the sun sets and the colours fade
it too reminds us that it's just another passing day

There is power in vulnerability.

You gather a strength
that would've never been obtained before
deriving intrinsically and will always be yours
a strength that is the purest form

Mr Melancholy

Dear Melancholy,

I rather enjoy to embrace and hold you dear
because you are there to hold my tears
for no particular reason
but simply there for me
oh how grateful and satisfied I can be

When I'm trapped in my shadow
when I've tripped and fallen
from the kerb of my thoughts
you are there to soften my fall

Somehow I find you when I least expect
somehow I find you often
somehow when I begin to hold you
the view clears, and I enjoy seeing the blue

Sometimes you are in the air just passing by
or prefer to spend a whole day by my side
but you are there holding my hand
as I begin to fall apart
maybe feeling lonely isn't so bad
because I have you,
Melancholy

On this journey, on *your* journey,
you will only run into what's *destined* for you

A logophile

Walloping words
bruise my heart
yet
sooth my soul

How the letters caress
my fingers
the words
hold my hand
a sentence
pulls my arm
out of my socket

Words
rip me raw
unleashing me
to the depths
of my soul

I have harnessed my power
to feel the sounds
and listen to the views
to taste the sweetness of a touch
(maybe I just sense too much)

But I am proud
how my soul sparkles
because it's dark
deep

down

I hold you back
yet wonderfully
pull you forward

—*Hope*

Torn in two or three or more

Action has taken toll
my thoughts suffocating the chair
on a desk made of dull

Listen to the brain
but nothing feels love
like my heart for arts

My veins
have turned to dust
my mind a muzz

Filling myself
with biscuits
I feel sick

At least
my face is washed
with salty water

My one heart
has multiple
lovers

I
have
too
many
passions

Practice makes progress
and patience is key
to be happy in life
and to enjoy the journey

The way of the world is weird and wonderful
don't just take the rails, walk your trails

Oh how I can take you
to wonderful places
no body ever could
yet you face brutality with me
our wars can always be fatal
you bear my weights
but soar through my glory
I am the most mighty thing you have
in fact
I am the most powerful thing
in this universe

—*Your brain*

Smile through the rain
breathe the air of the storm
you too will feel restored

All you need to do
is embrace the actuality
of what's going on
and find the beauty within
to flow with life

The Sapling

Someone once
called me a sapling
I was new
to the written art
but a 'sapling'
suggests I'll get far

I ask myself
how much I'll see
or
how much I'll be seen
oak, cherry blossom, coast redwood
yet it's through the depths of my roots
I shall only be understood

I breathe the air of time
and one will surely find
how its precious presents
is rather sublime

Though the fuel to flourish
like pollen to spring
is this thing

Patience

Steering the sapling
to the highest of heights
it's bound to attain

About the author

Tess Lina Aiteouakrim is a poet and musician born and raised in London. She uses poetry as her best attempt to describe the indescribable and takes inspiration from the everyday. As a current student of science, Tess particularly enjoys fusing her passions of science and art into pieces to uncover the depths and truths of the world which we live in. Tess has had her poetry previously published in journal magazines and will continue to share her passions with people with the hope of bringing attention to the vital beauty of embracing all the wonders of the world.

Conscious Dreams
PUBLISHING

Transforming diverse writers
into successful published authors

www.consciousdreamspublishing.com

authors@consciousdreamspublishing.com

Let's connect

Milton Keynes UK
Ingram Content Group UK Ltd.
UKHW021824201223
434735UK00013B/856